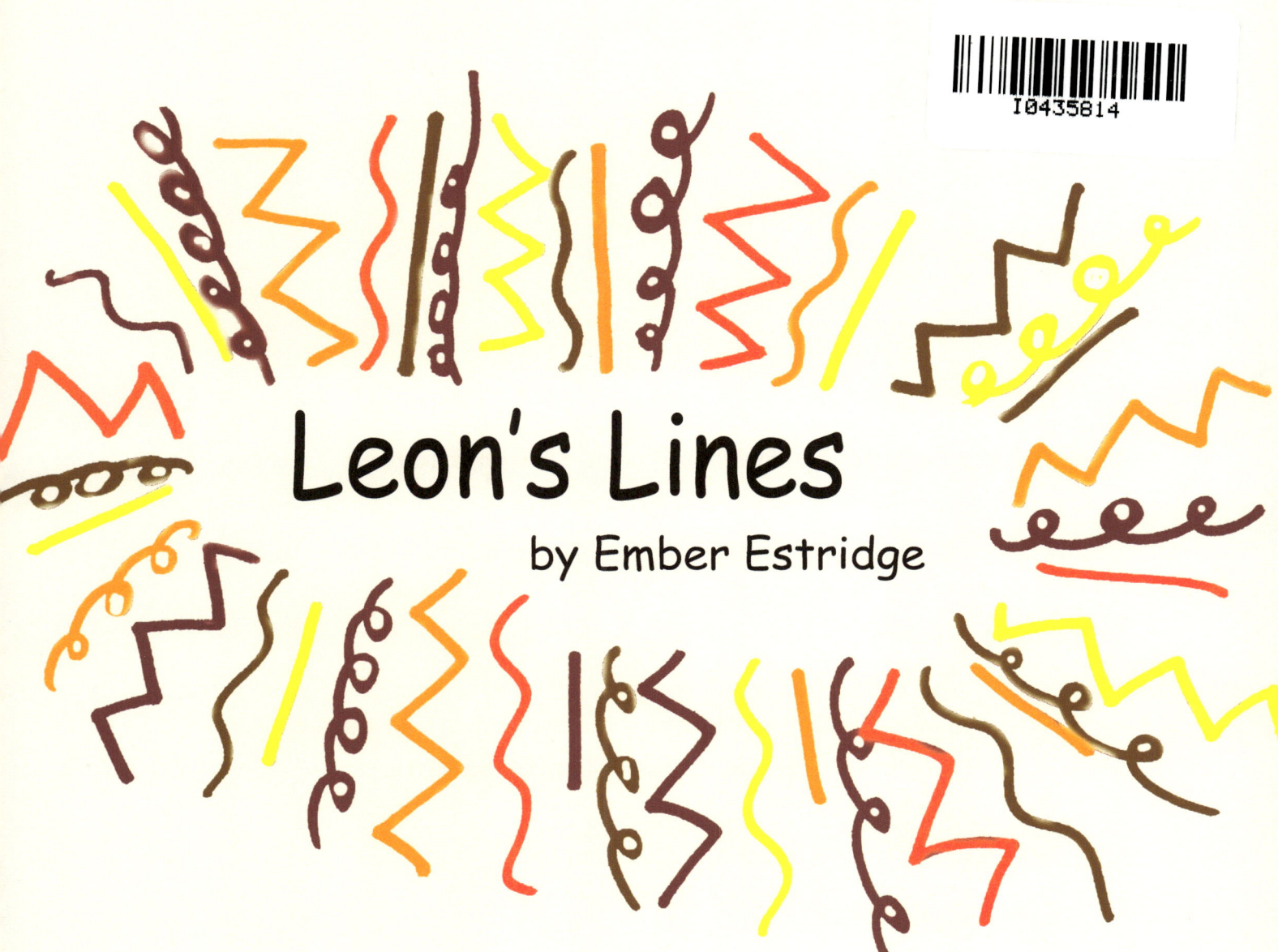

Leon's Lines

by Ember Estridge

Martina Publishing, Inc.

South Carolina

Books may be purchased online in quantity and/or special sales
by contacting the author at estridgee2@mailbox.winthrop.edu.

Book Summary: Leon, the lion, discovers one of the elements of design by drawing lines and enhancing his artwork to make beautiful art.

Martina Publishing, Inc.
www.ShielaMartina.com

ISBN-13: 978-0-9799344-2-1
Library of Congress Control Number: 2016919334

[1. Art—Fiction. 2. Element of design—Lines. 3. Animals—Lion.] I. Title.
First Edition
Printed in the United States of America

Dedication

I dedicate this book to all minds ready to learn and create.

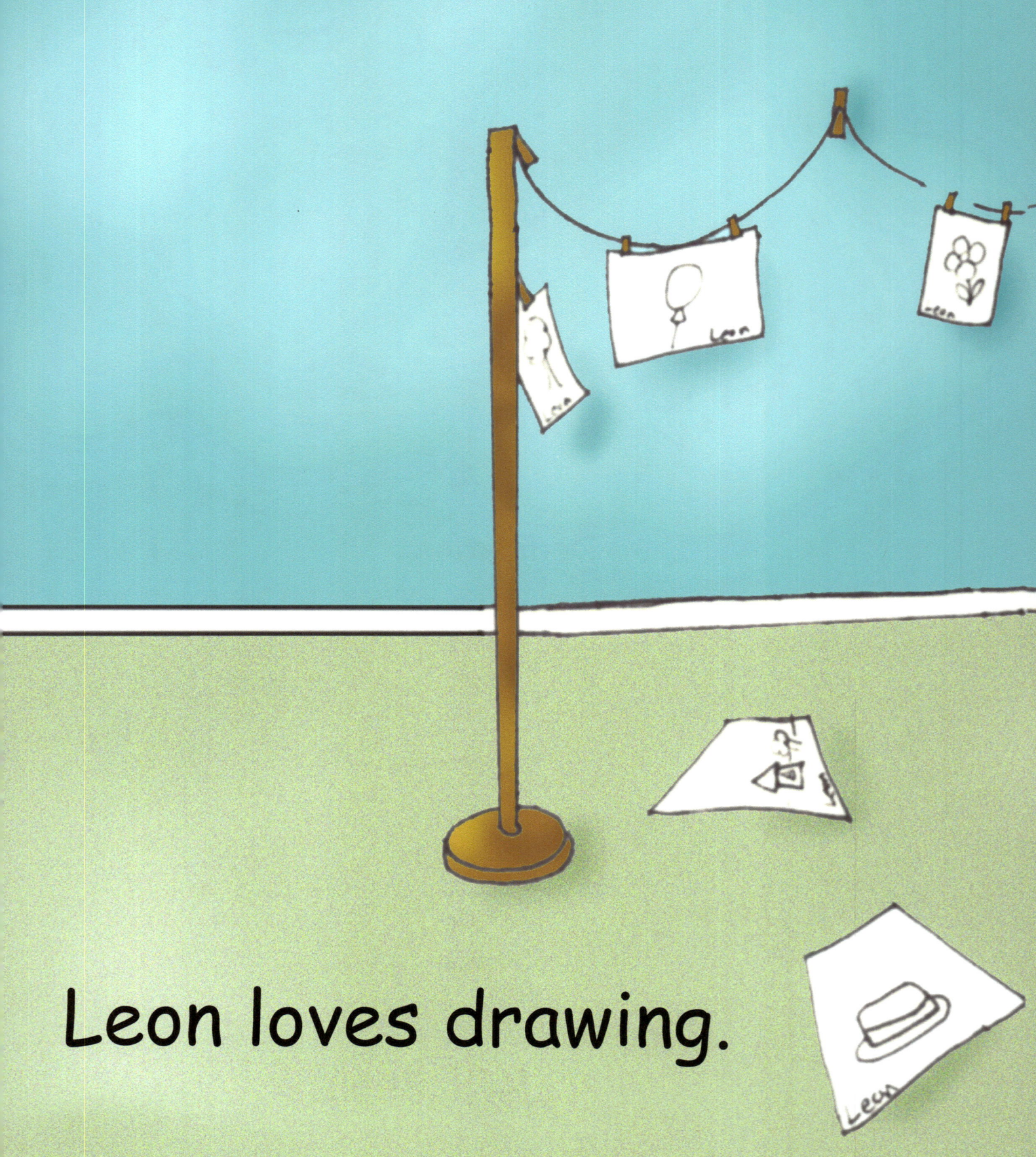

Leon loves drawing.

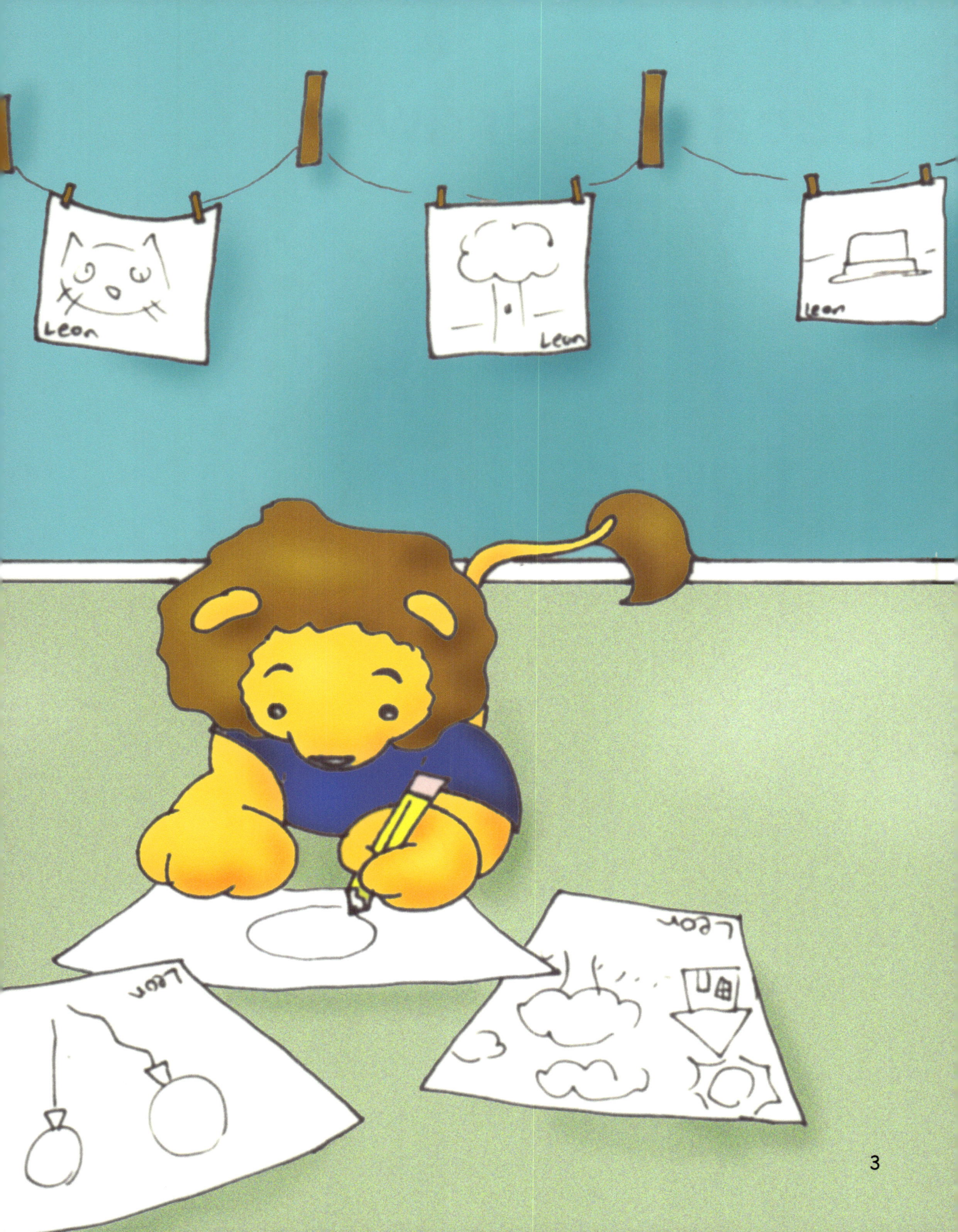

Leon can draw
many things.

flowers

cats

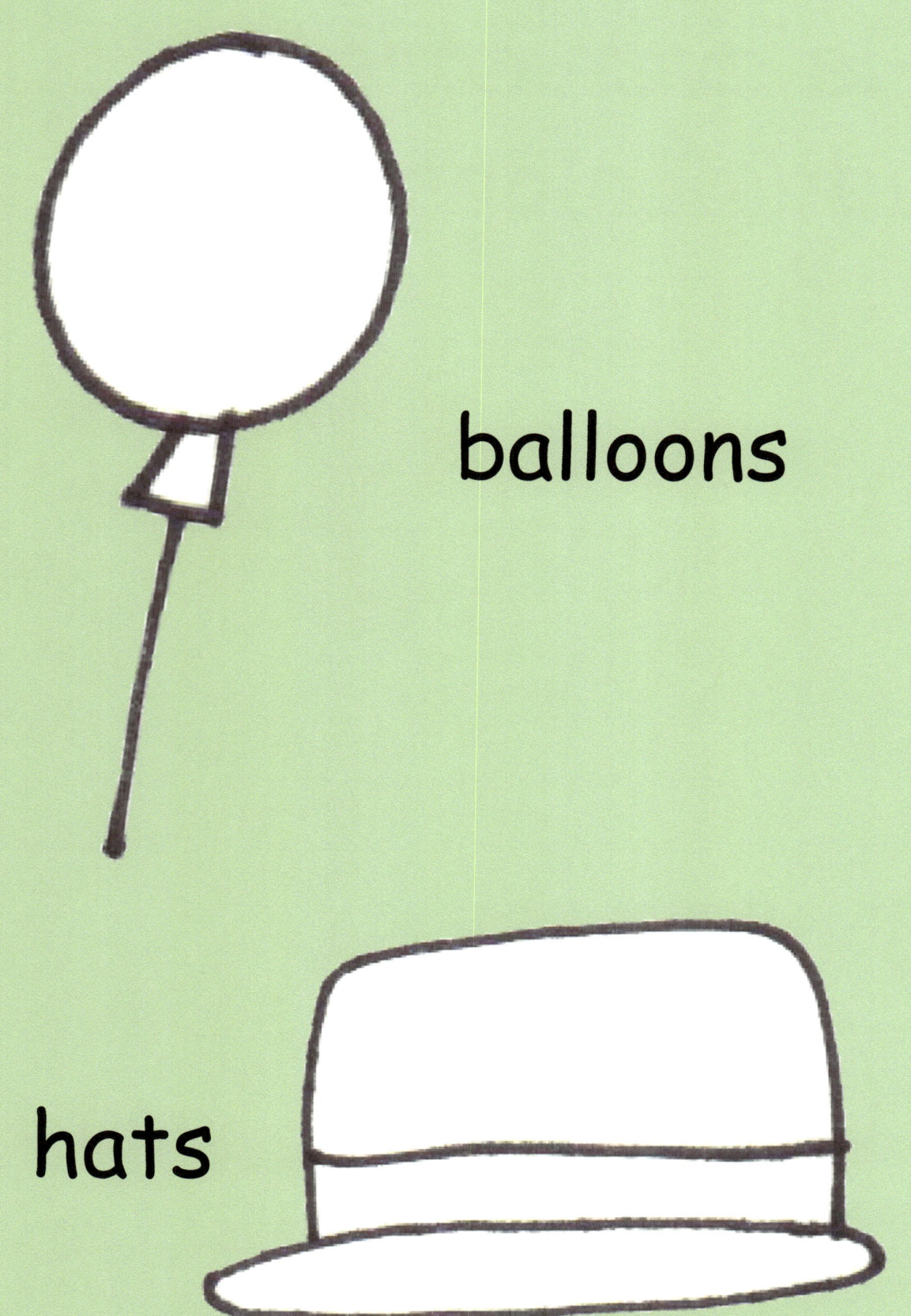

balloons

hats

He even carefully
adds colors.

RED
and
GREEN

ORANGE
and
BLUE

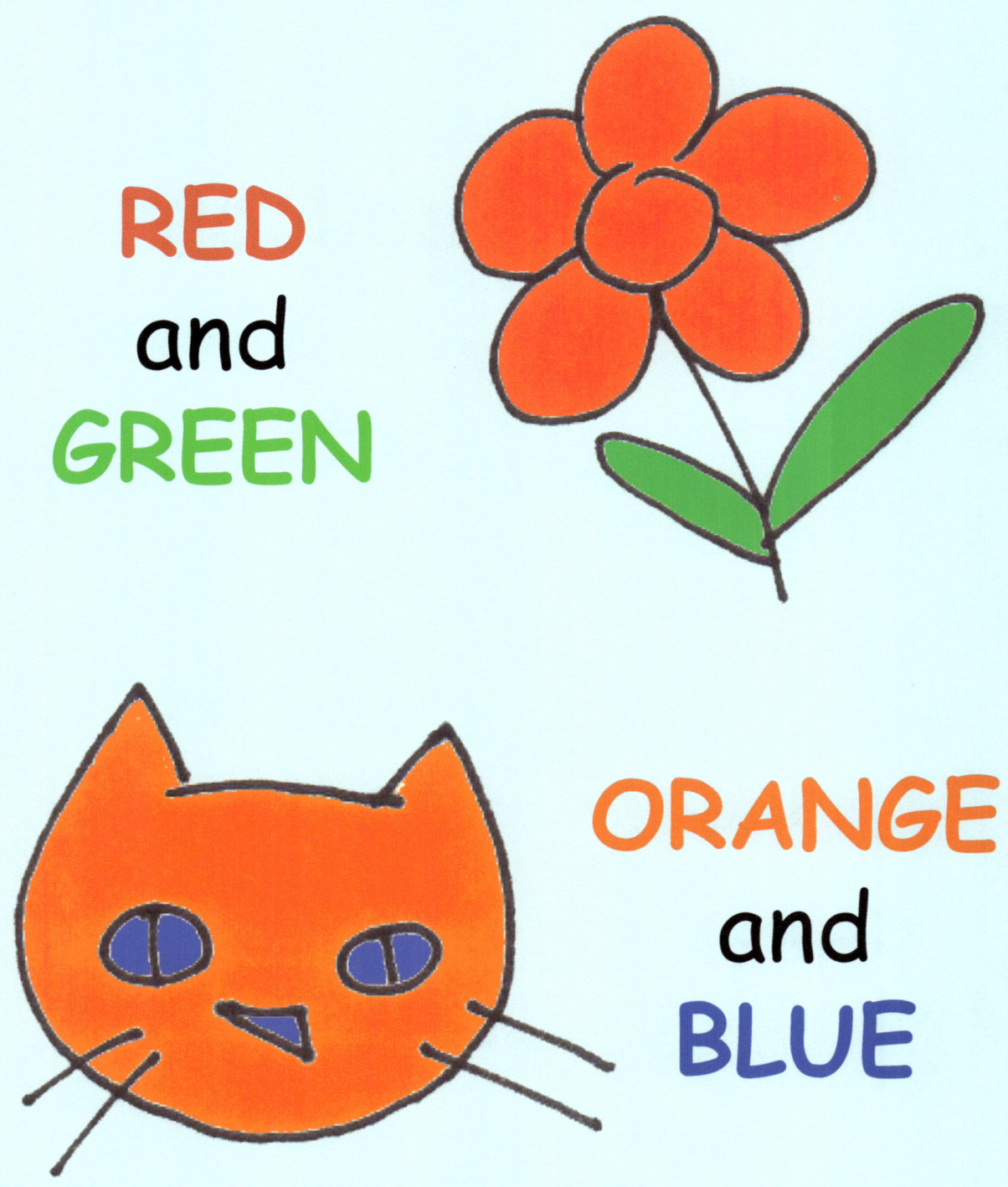

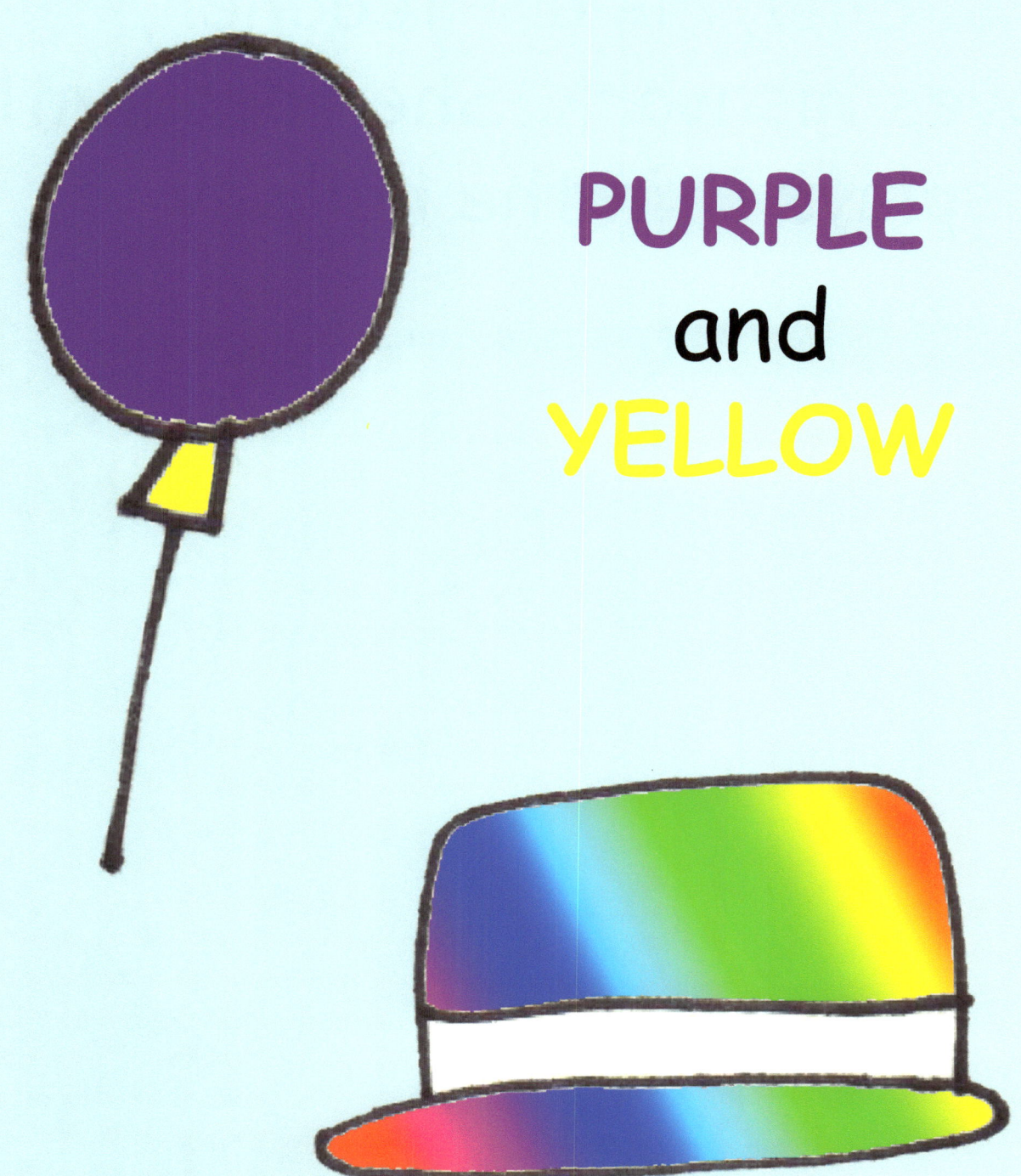

PURPLE
and
YELLOW

even the entire
RAINBOW

Ms. Emu, his art teacher, loves his work. She frequently displays it in the hallway.

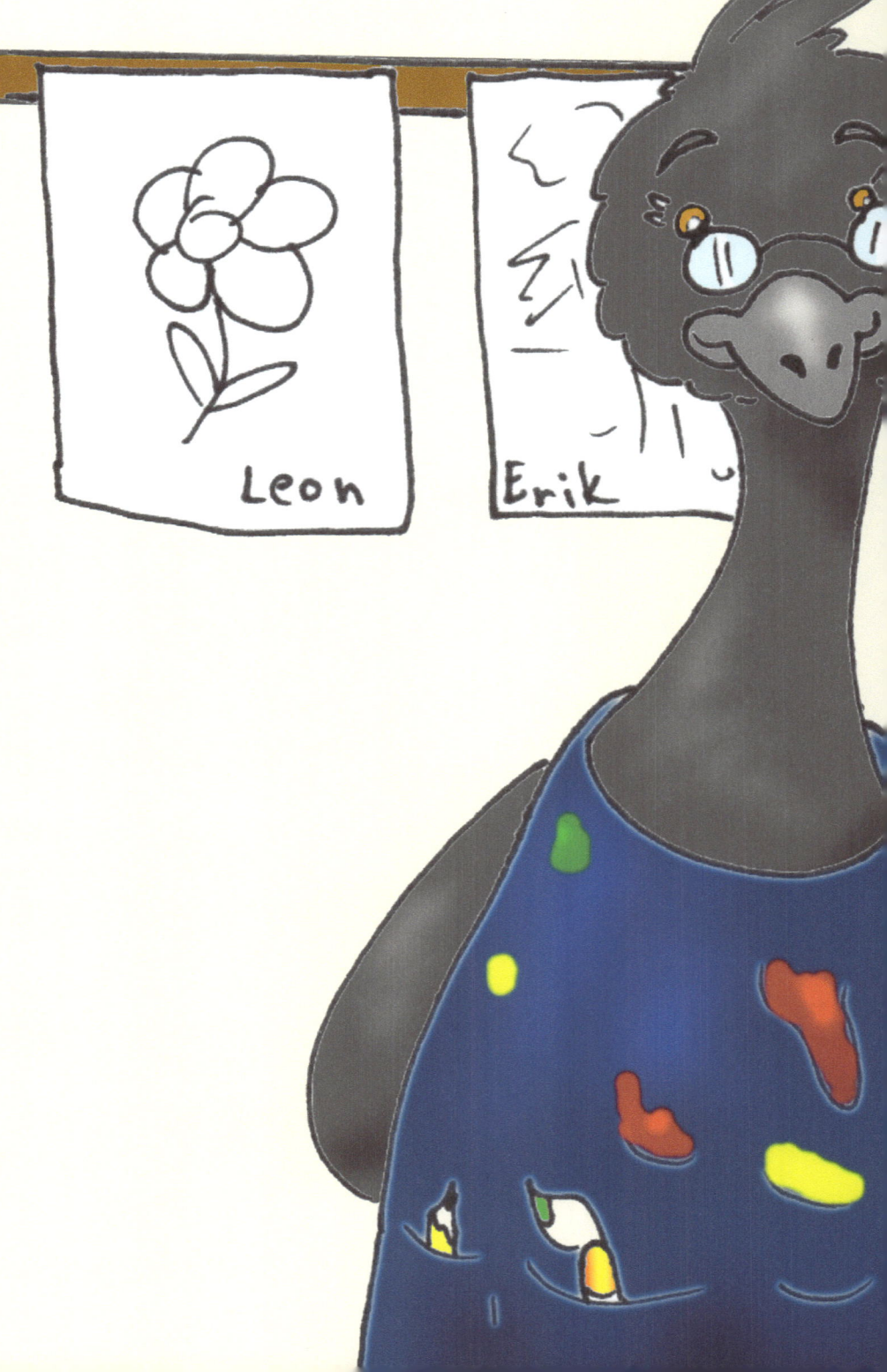

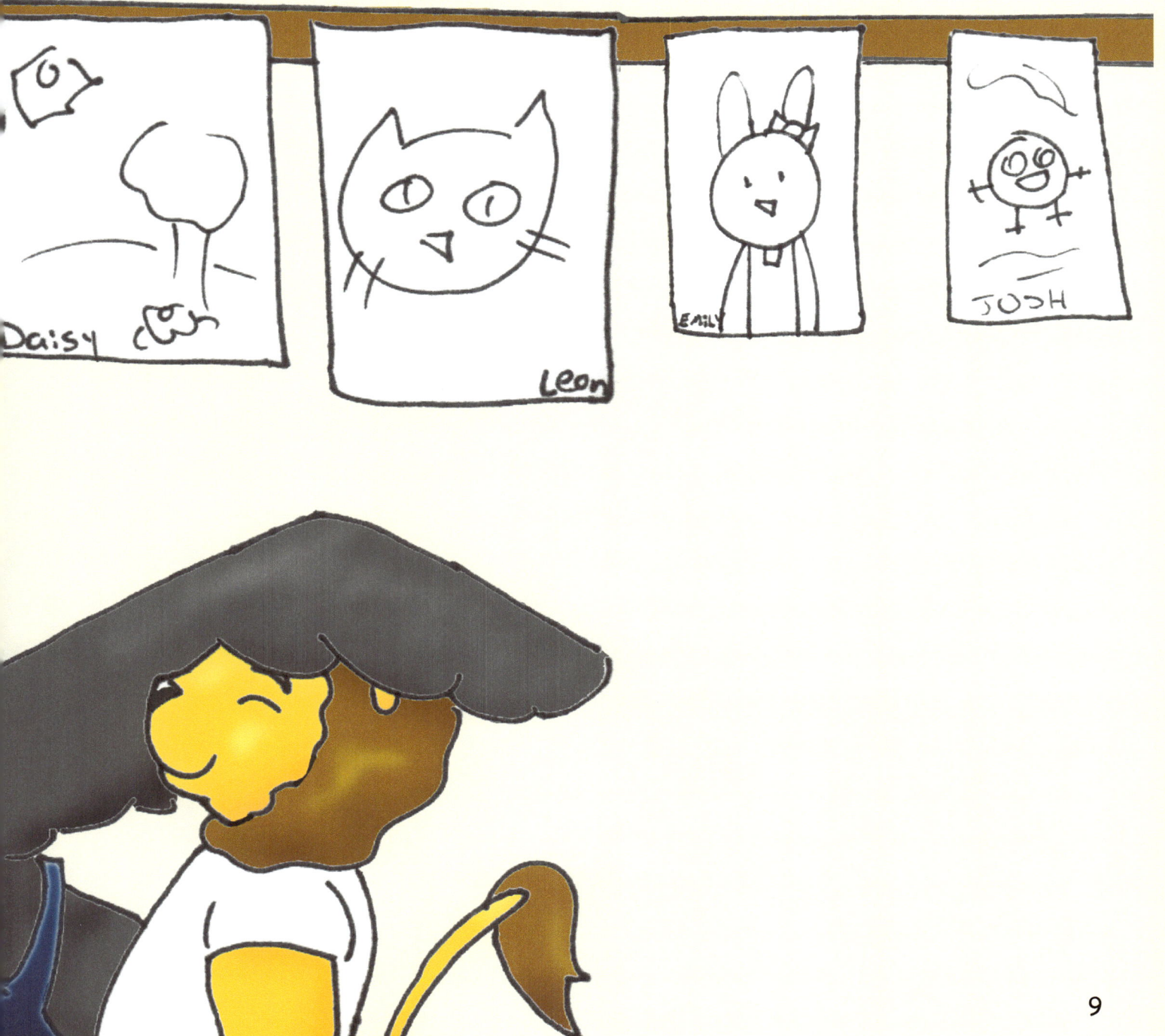

One day, Ms. Emu taught an element of design—

line.

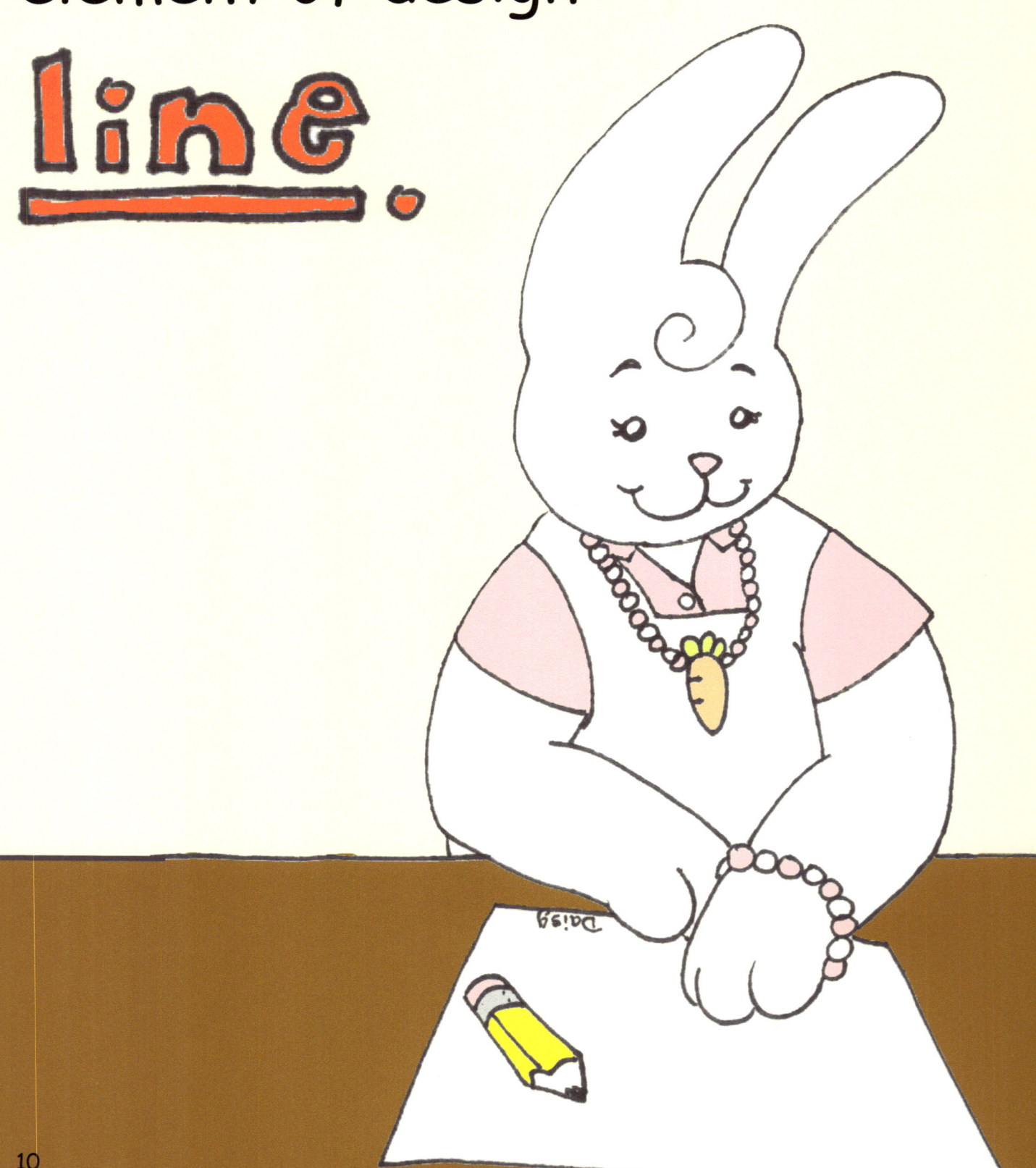

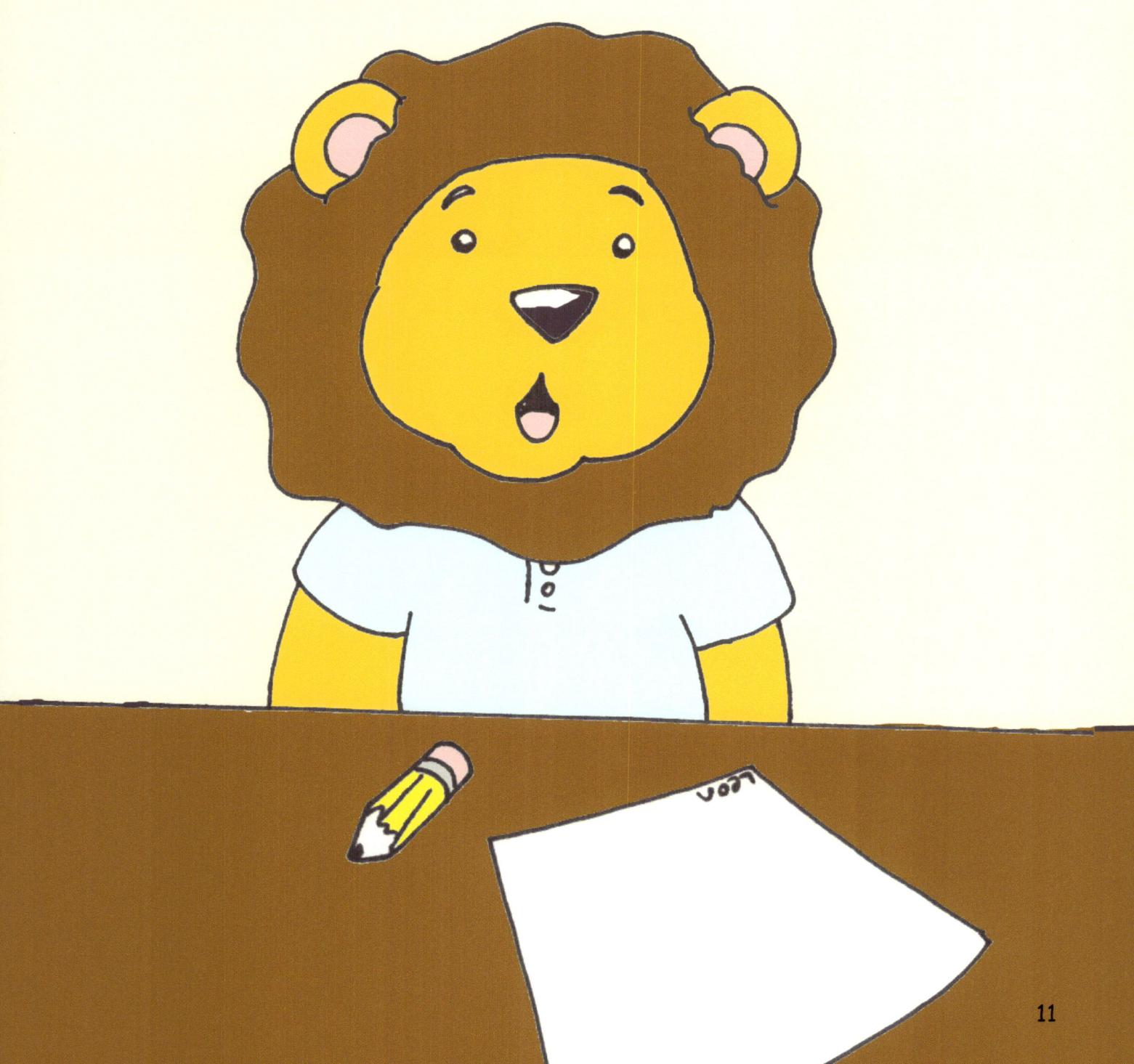

There are many kinds of lines.

thin lines

thick lines

straight lines

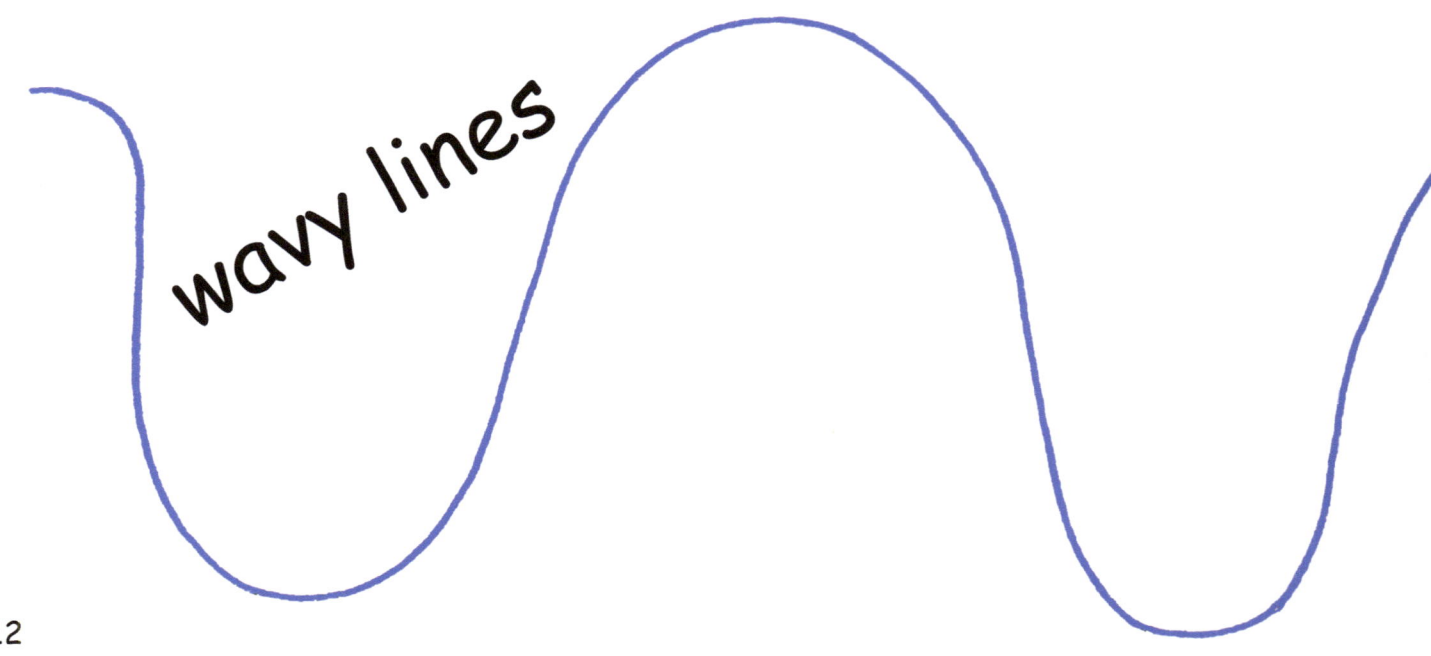

wavy lines

curly lines

13

zig zag lines

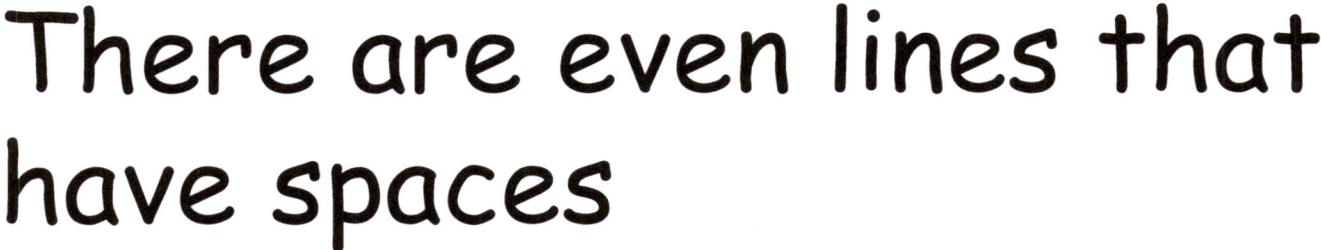

There are even lines that have spaces

like dashed lines

and dotted lines.

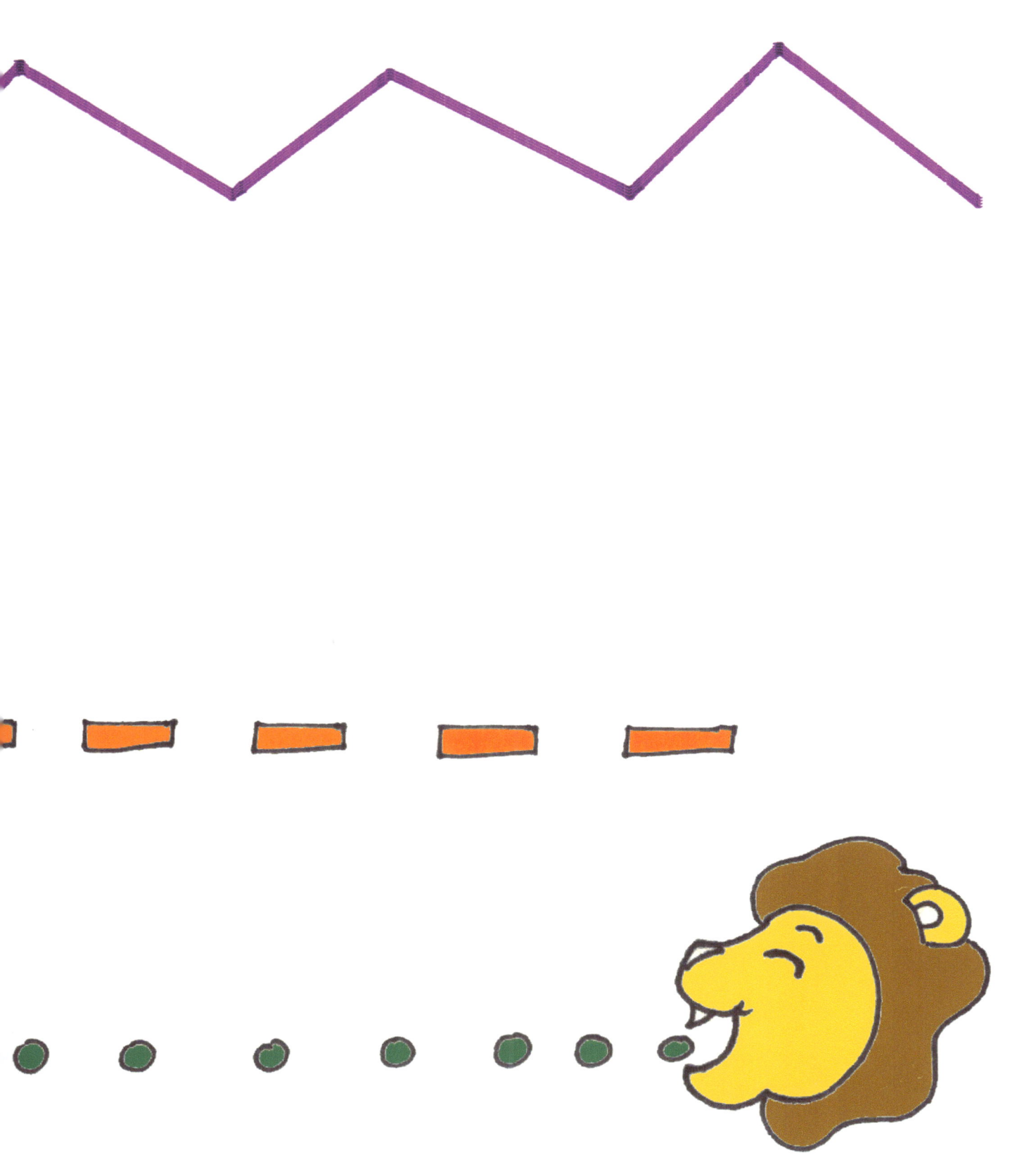

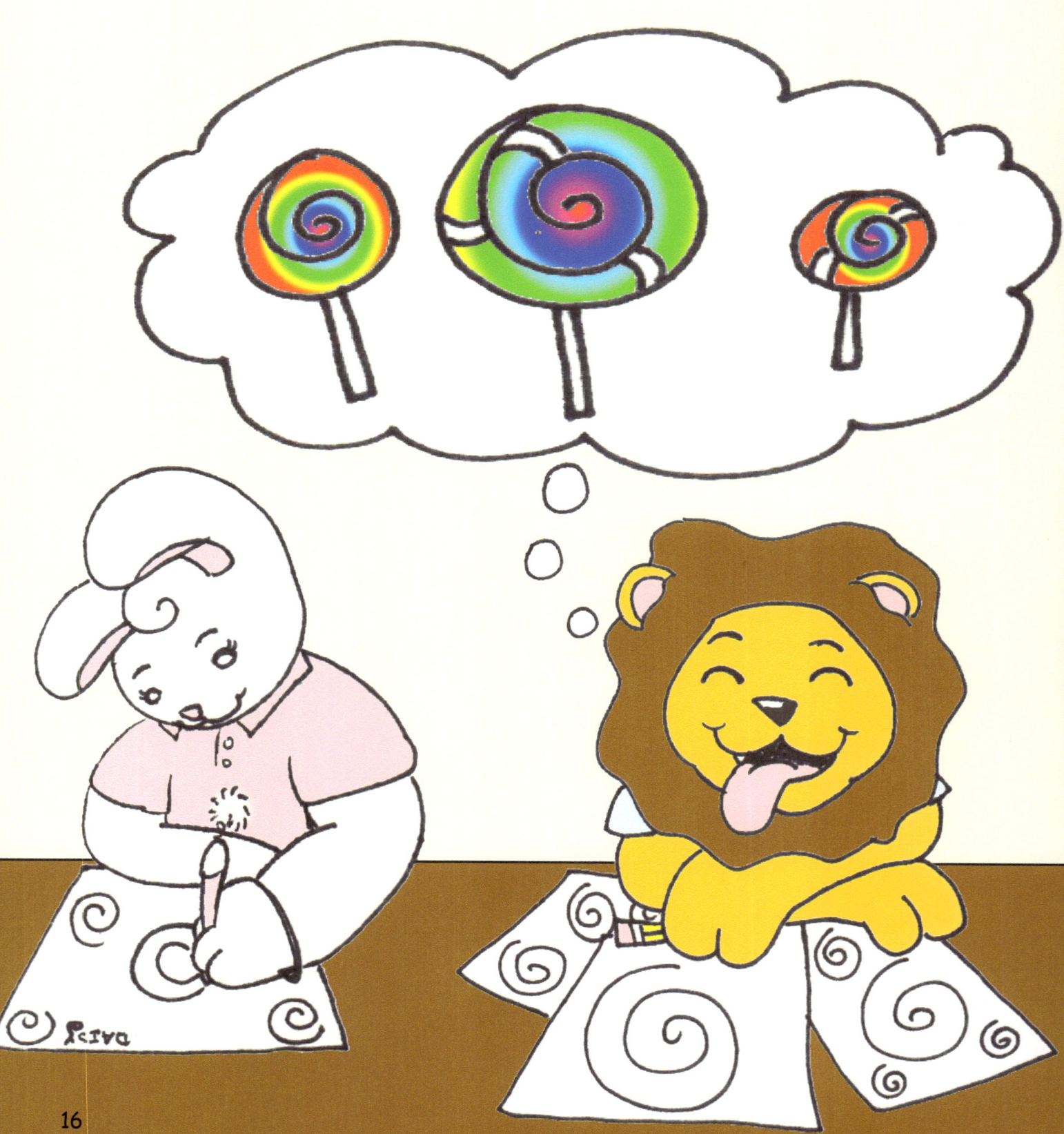

16

The swirl line was Leon's favorite. It reminded him of his favorite candy, lollipops.

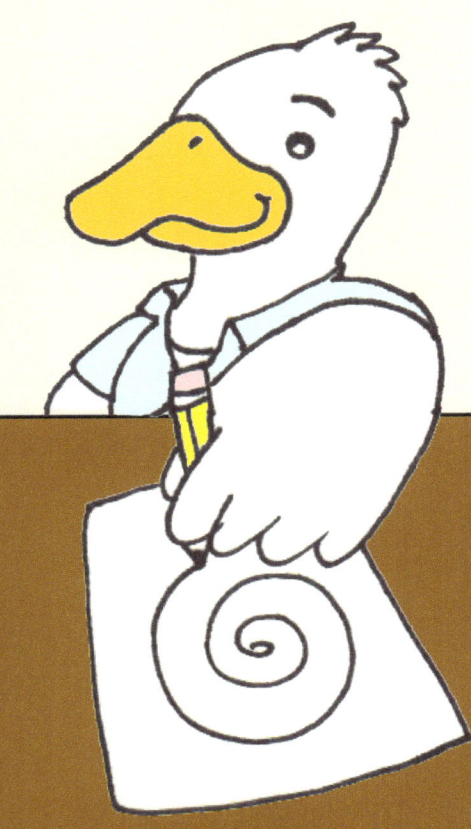

Leon went home and
practiced drawing his lines.
He even added them
to his pictures!

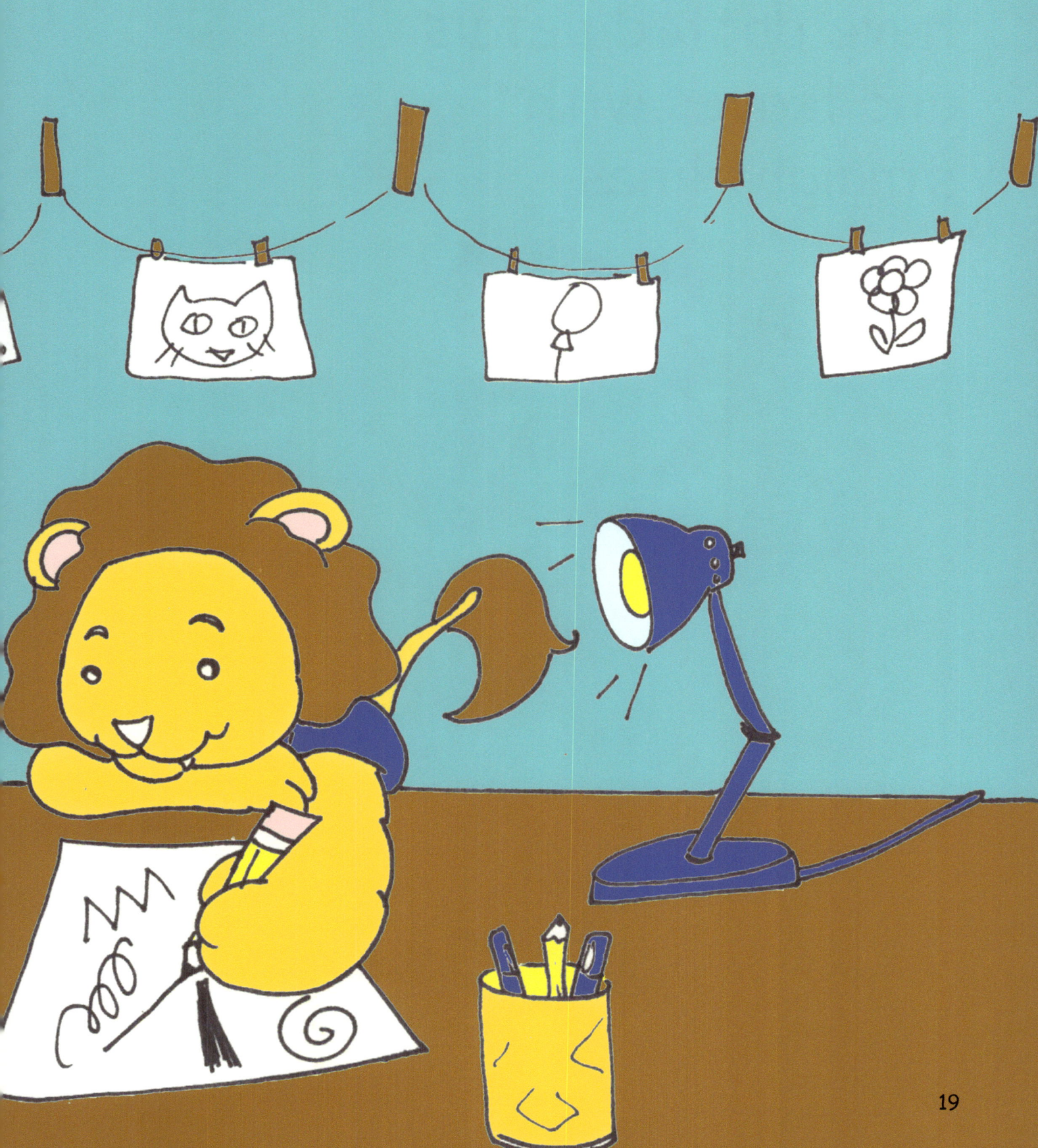

Leon's flowers now
have dotted petals
and leaves with
straight lines.

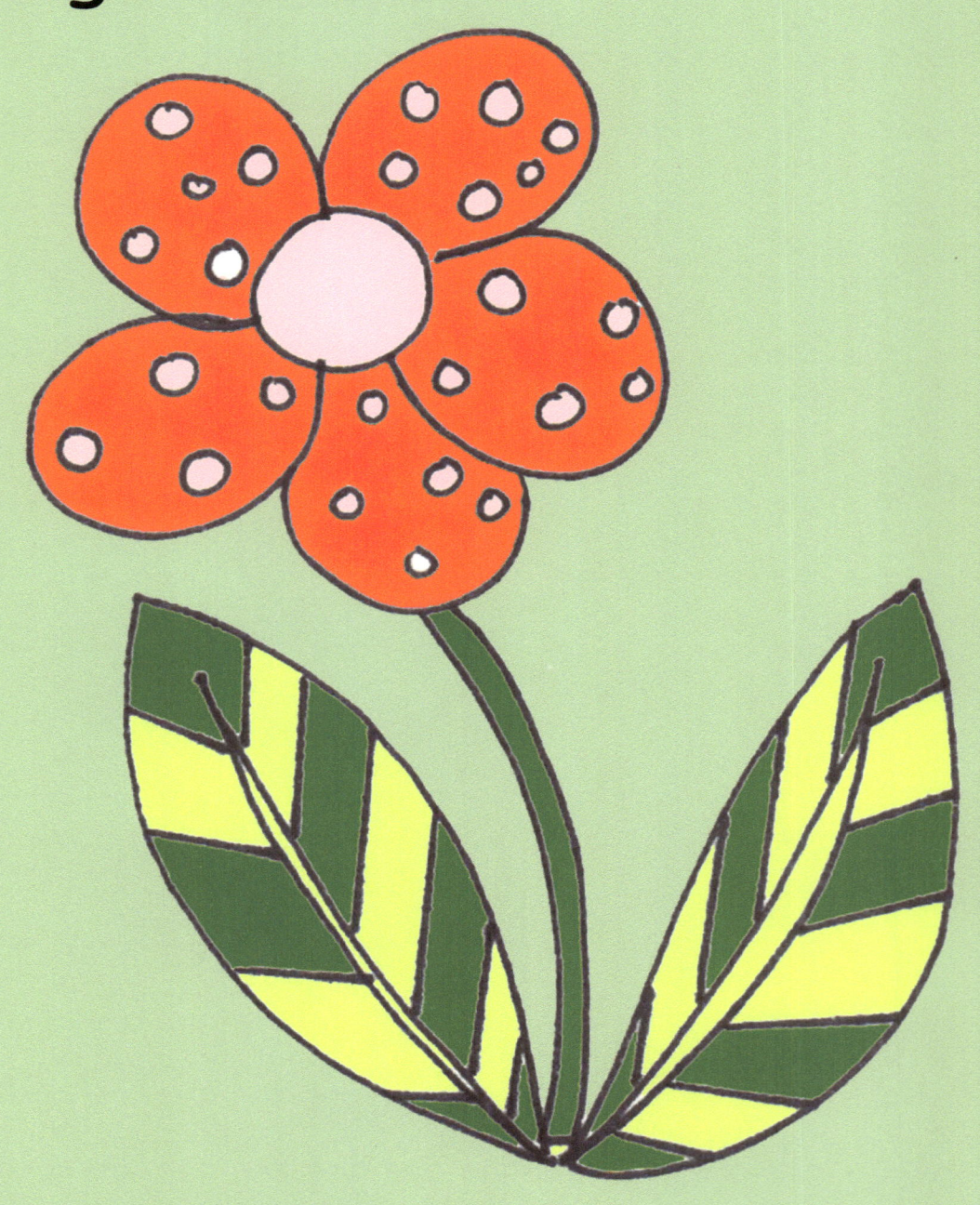

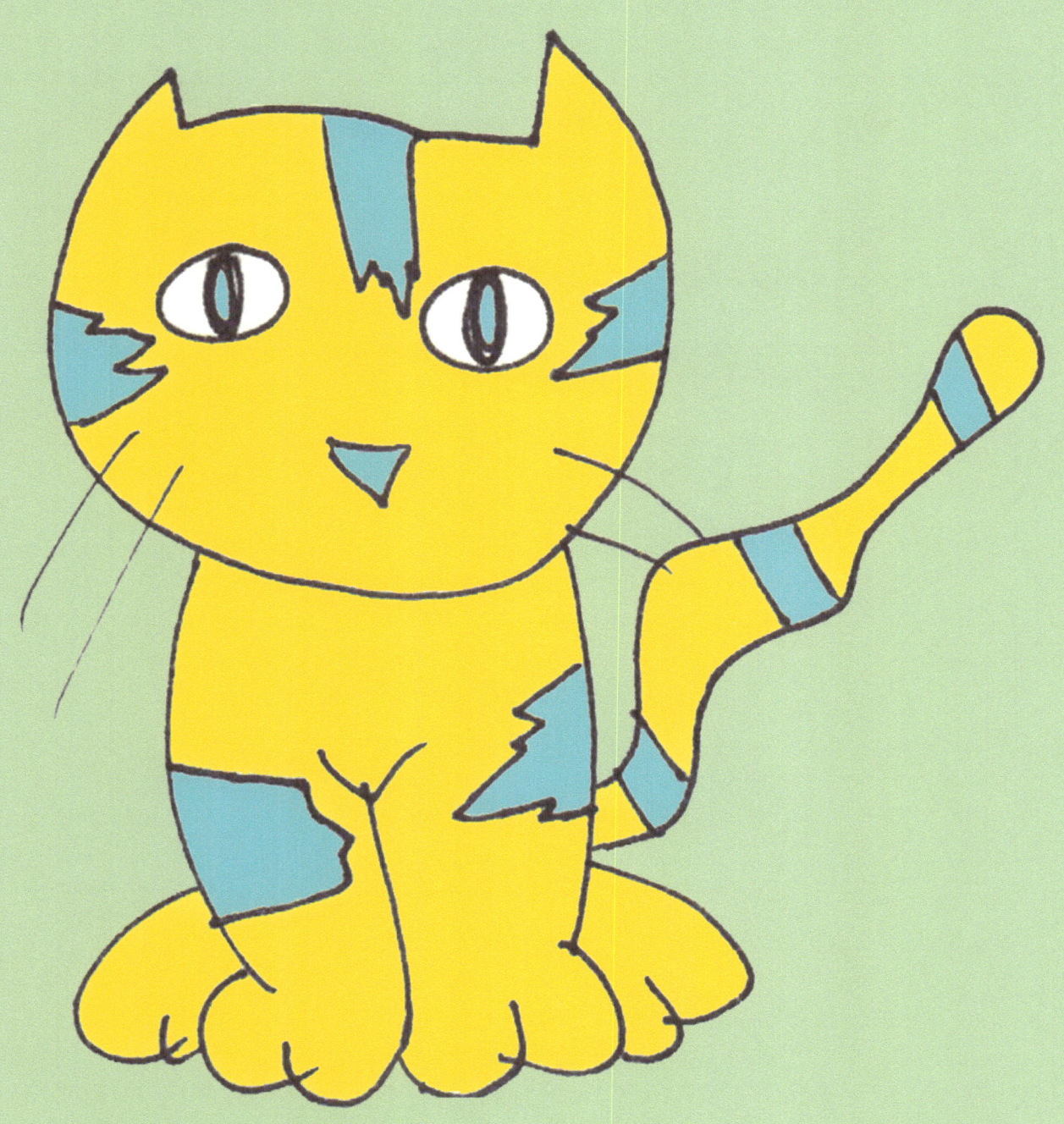

His cats now have
thick stripes and
wavy tails.

His balloons now have zigzags and curly strings.

His hats now have
dashed lines everywhere.

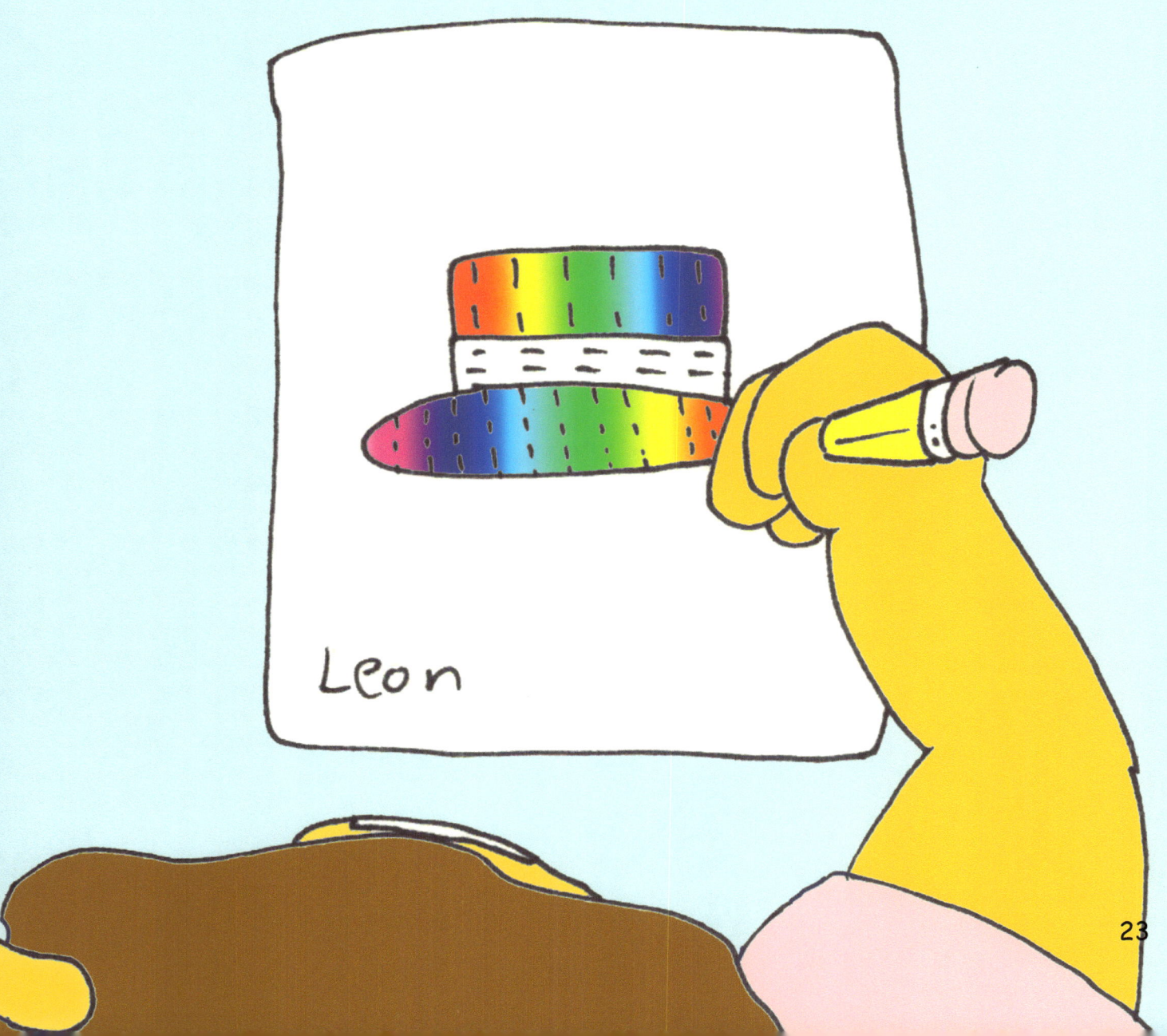

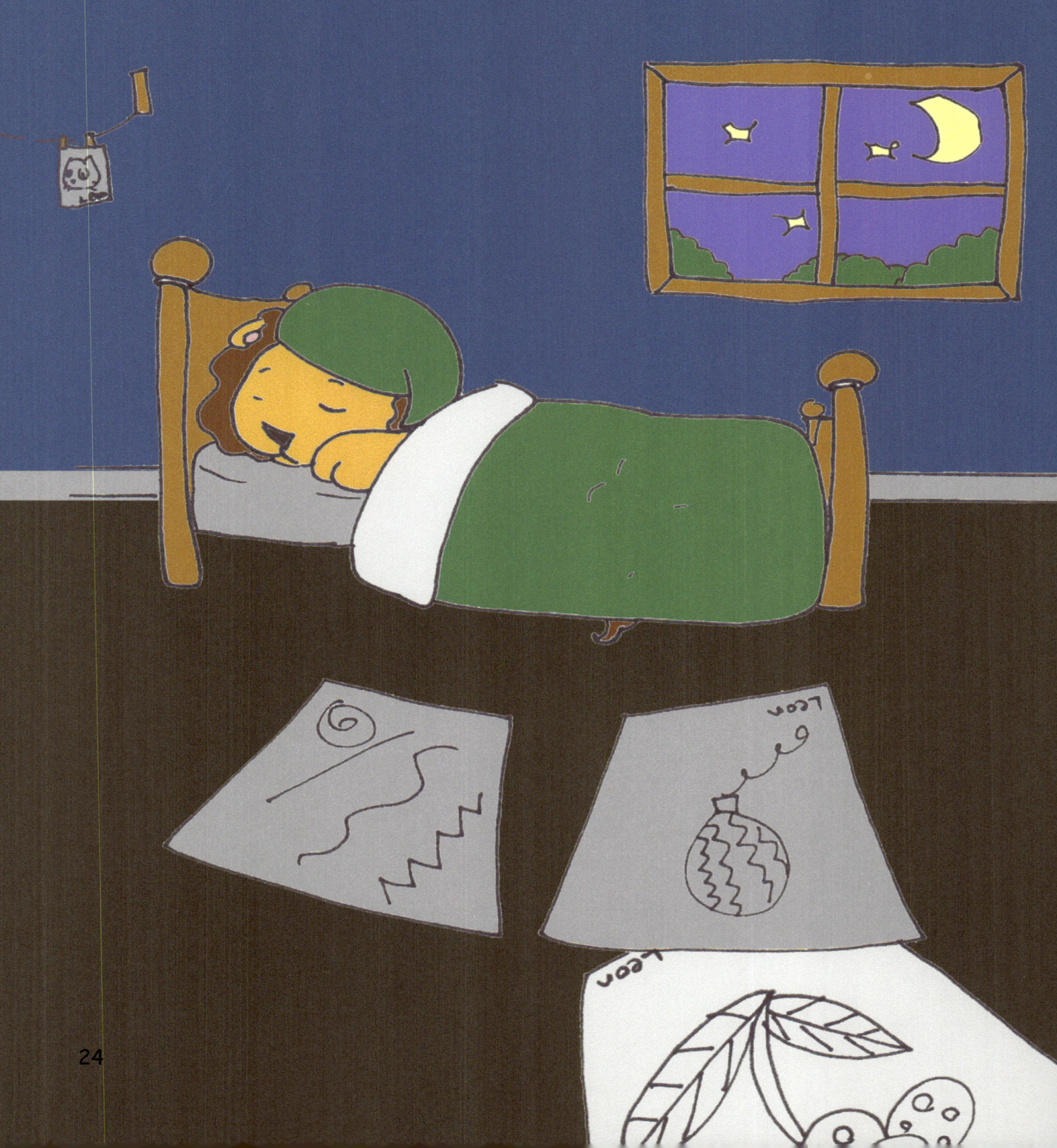

Leon draws until bedtime,
and lines fill his dreams.

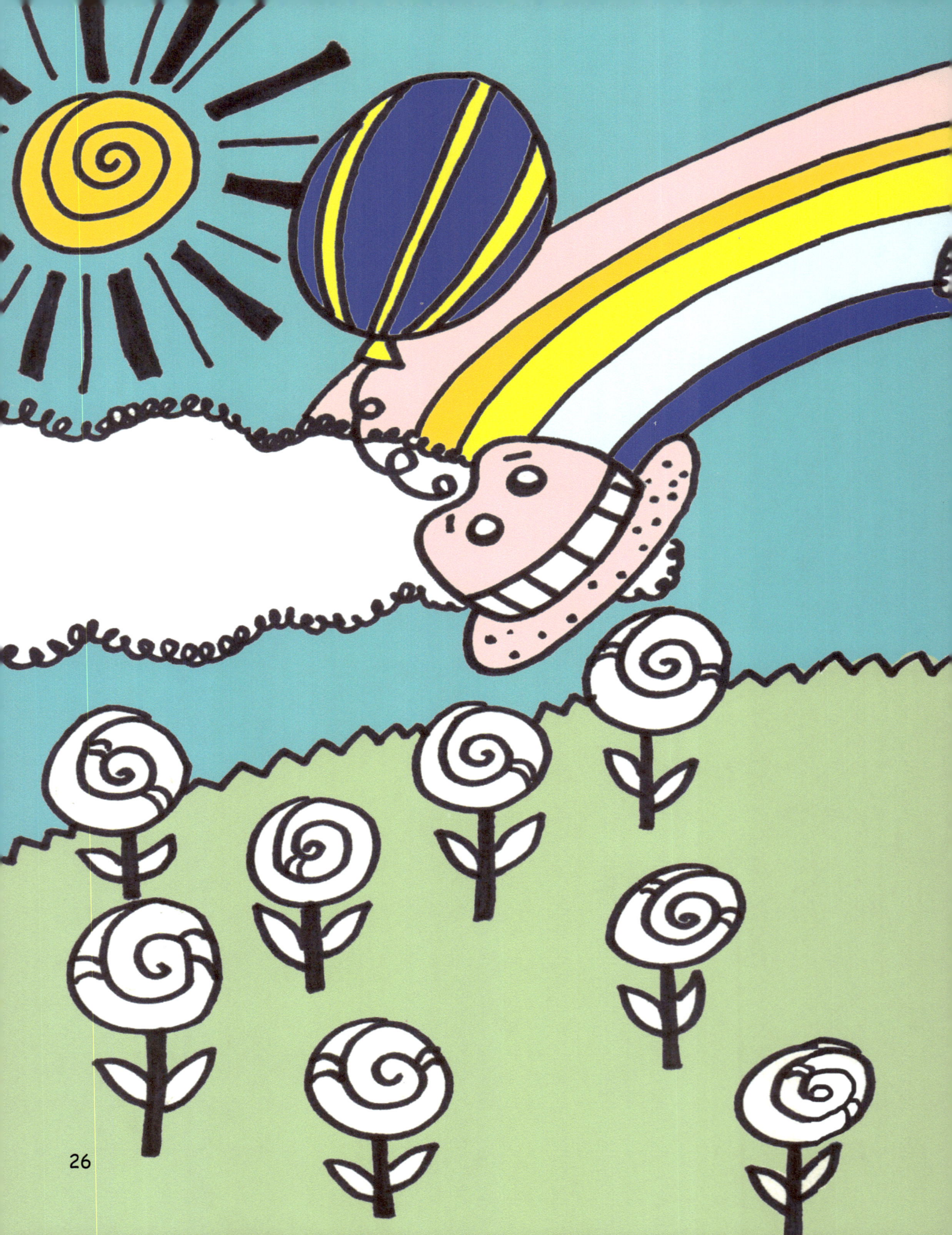

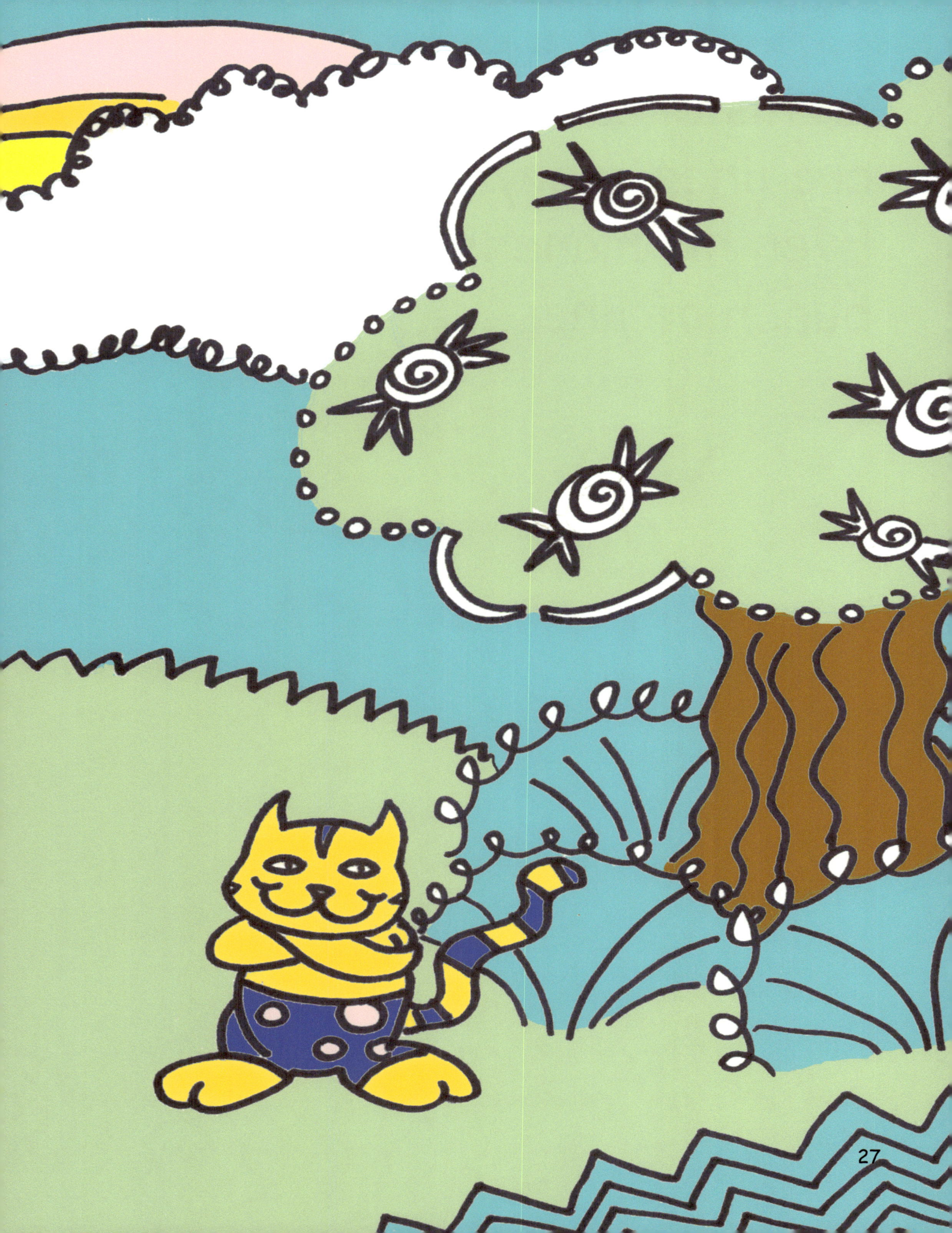

In his dreams, there
are lines everywhere.
Even his mane is a
bunch of lines.

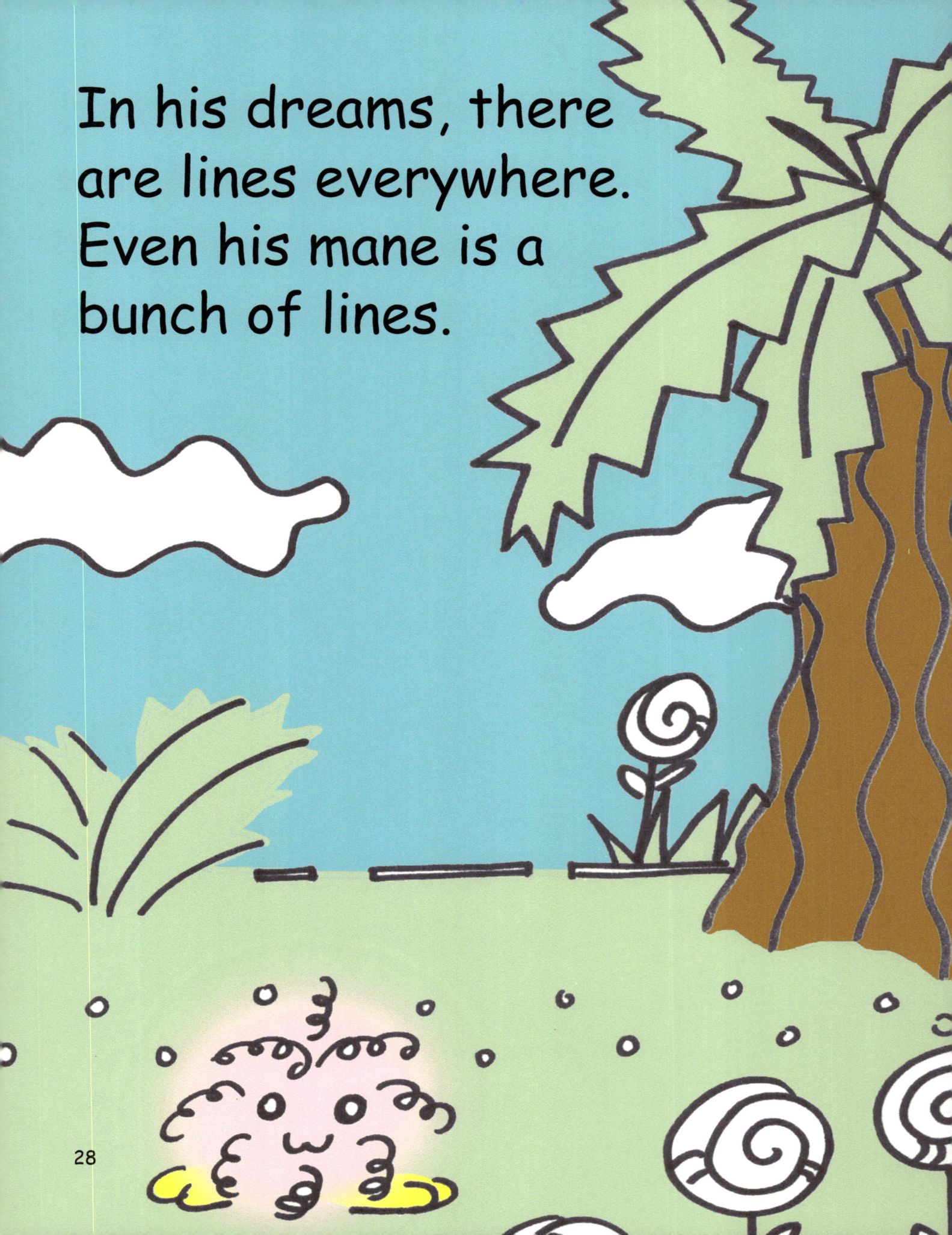

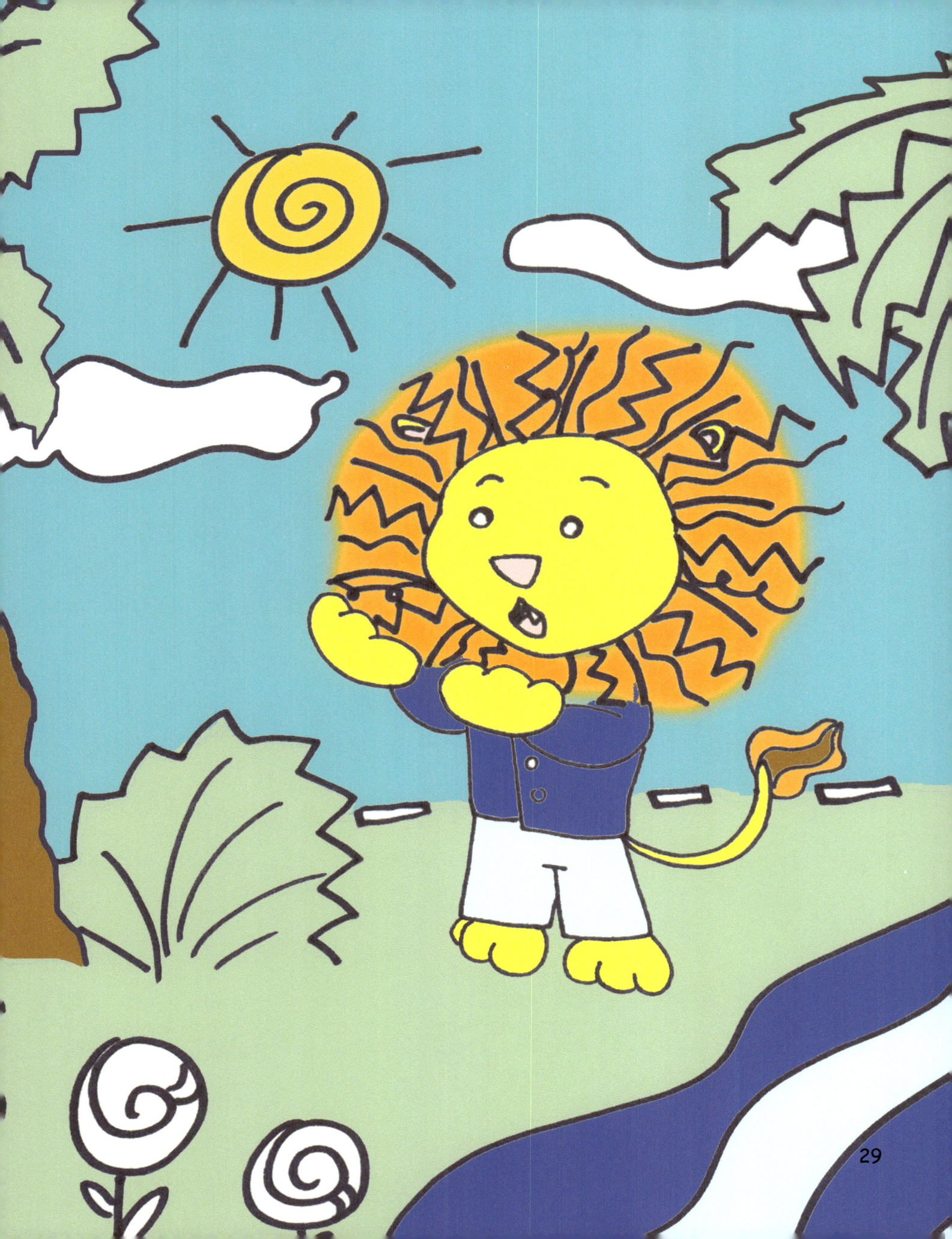

29

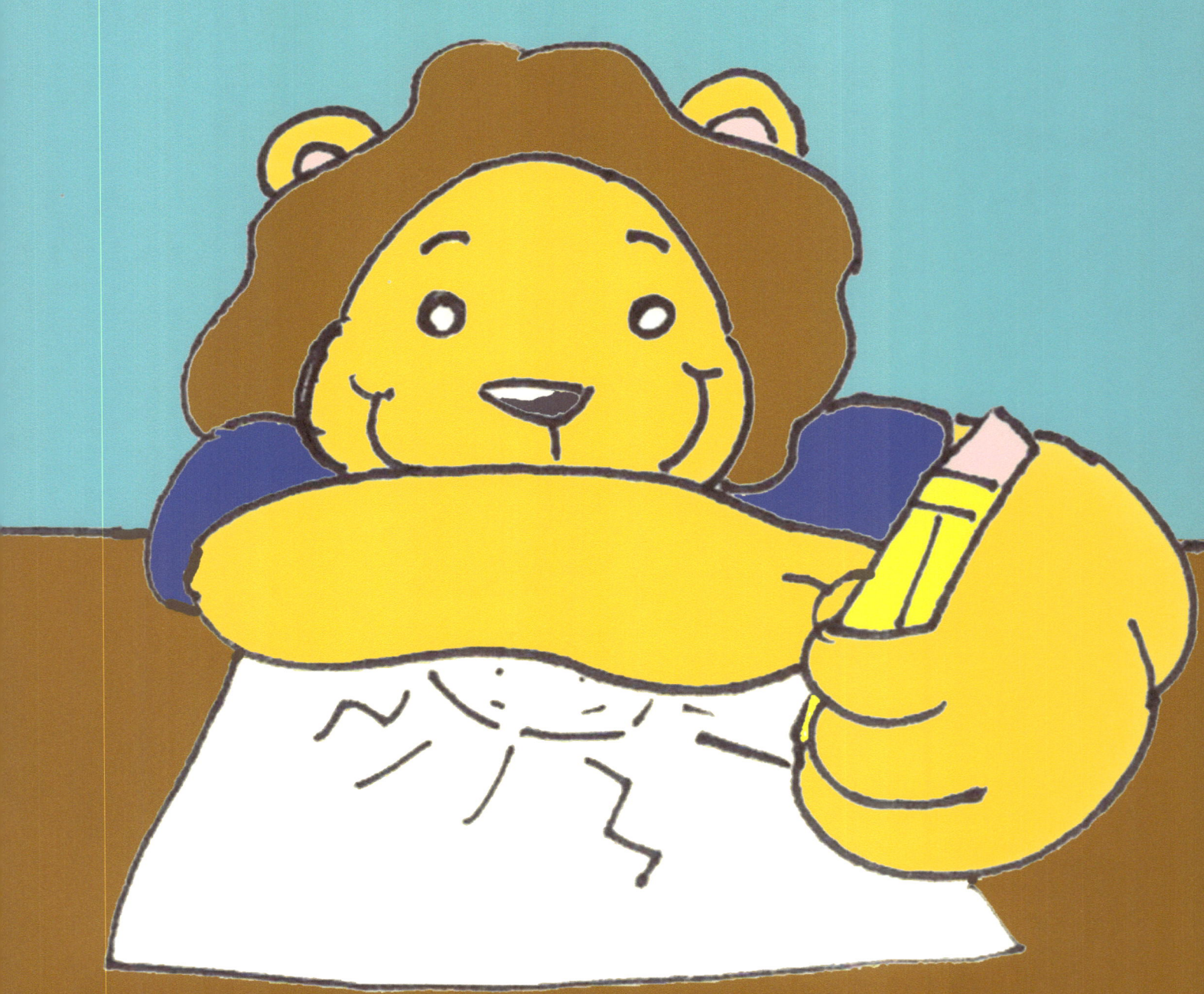

In the morning, Leon draws a self portrait using different lines for his mane just like in his dream.

Leon hangs it proudly on his wall.

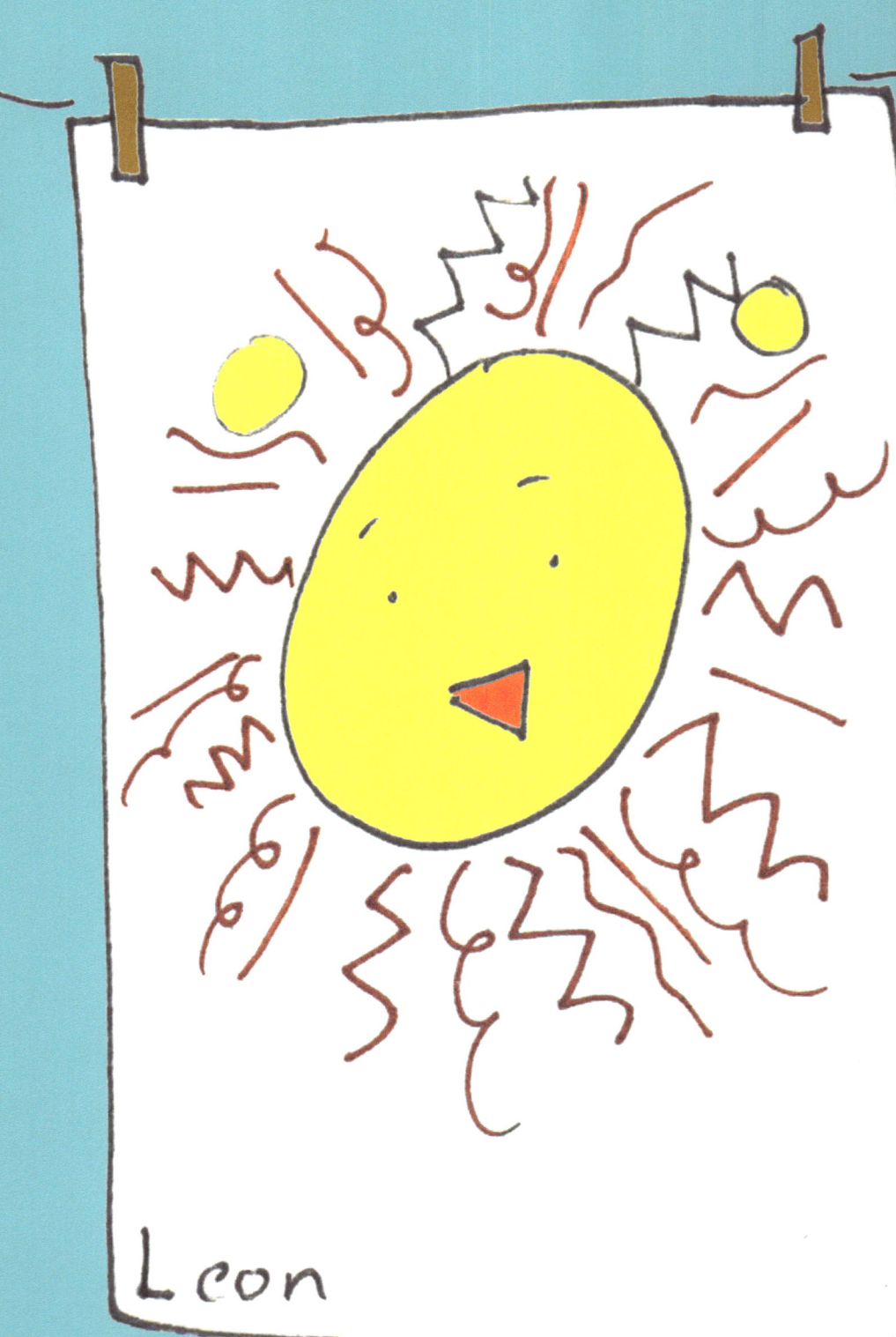

Leon

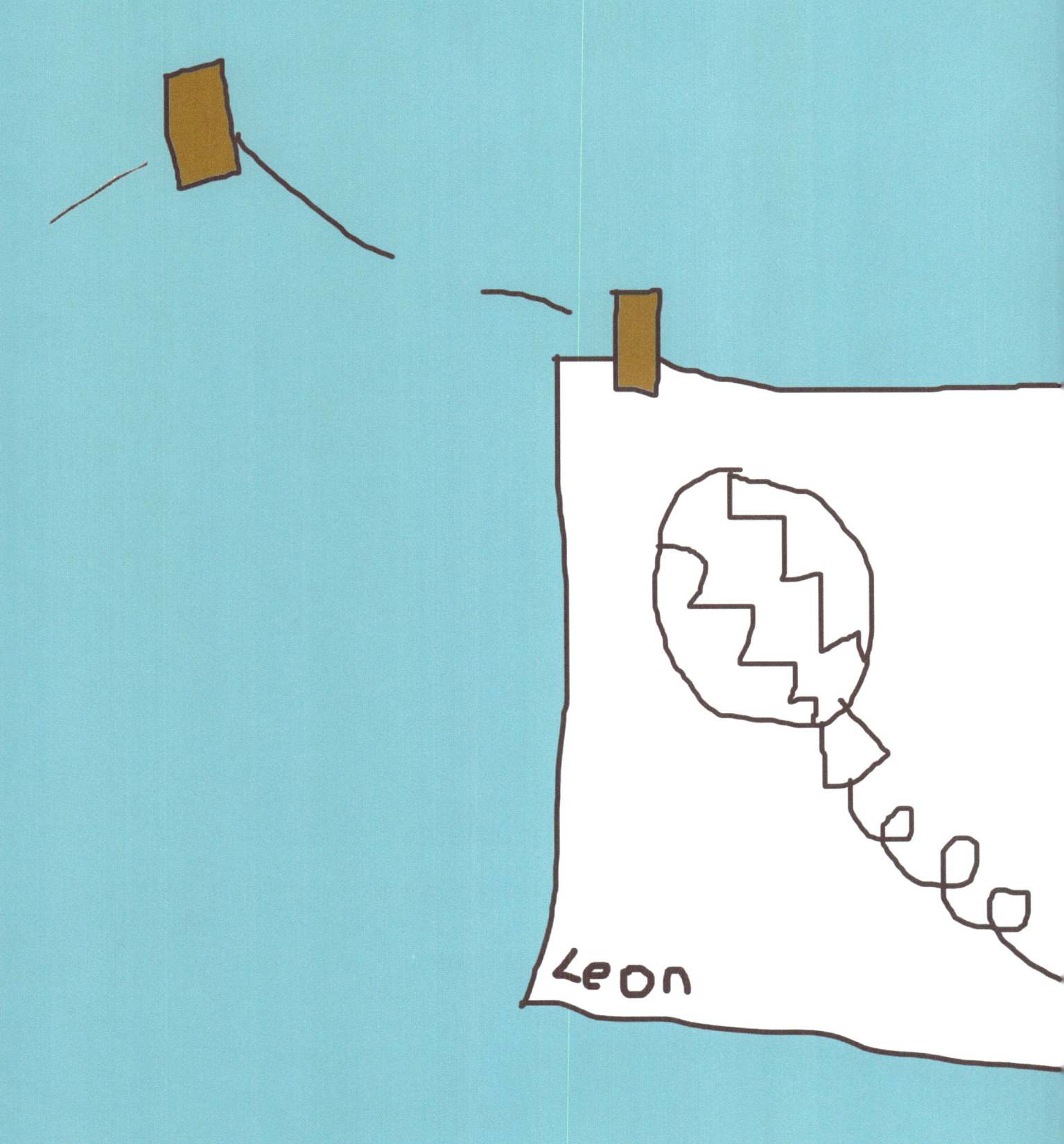

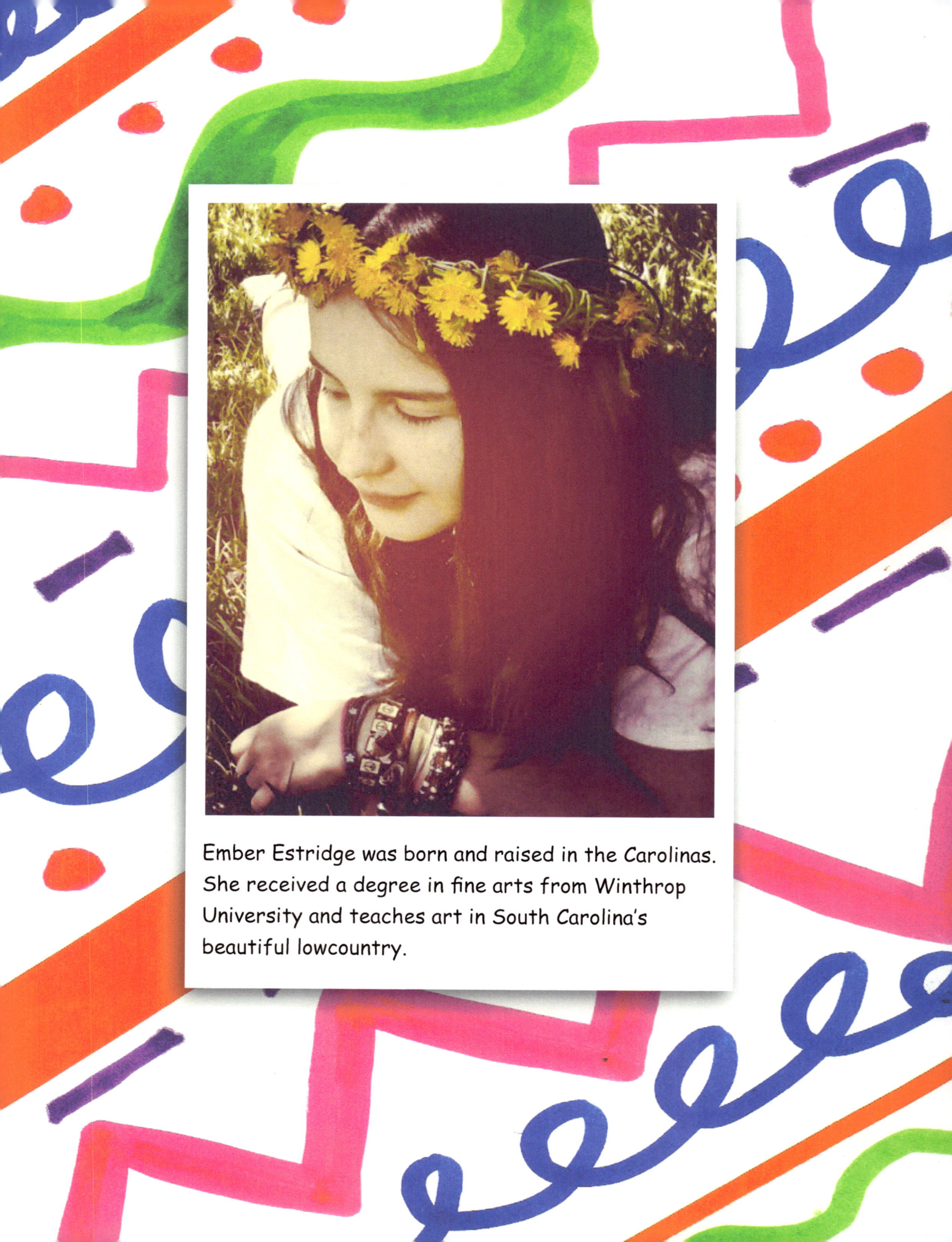

Ember Estridge was born and raised in the Carolinas. She received a degree in fine arts from Winthrop University and teaches art in South Carolina's beautiful lowcountry.

www.ingramcontent.com/pod-product-compliance
Lightning Source LLC
Chambersburg PA
CBHW060839290526
45792CB00006BB/1993